BUMPS IN THE ROAD

STEVE WOODS

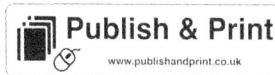
Publish & Print
www.publishandprint.co.uk

The right of Steve Woods to be identified as the author of **Bumps In The Road** has been asserted by him under Copyright Amendment (Moral Rights) Act 1998.

All rights reserved.

Copyright © Steve Woods 2024.

No part of this publication may be reproduced, stored in or introduced into a retrieval system or transmitted by any other form or by any means without the prior written consent of the author. Also, this book may not be hired out whether for a fee or otherwise in any cover other than supplied by the author.

ISBN: 9798337639765

All photographs: Steve and Sue Woods

All words that come to mind are inadequate,

yet they must be called upon, sometimes, to serve

Thanks to those who couldn't and those who wouldn't

for inspiring the belief that I can

Contents

Bumps In The Road

Magical Reality

It was one of those days.
It was definitely one of those.
The neighbour's cat had shat,
on the landing of the opposite flat.
The sky was leaden.

The usual problem,
towards the arse end of life.
Too much time to kill; so ironic.
Not like him to rise so late,
he's usually up like a bull out of a gate.

Well, not quite, his routine is light.
But not today.
Today is shopping day.
He could catch a bus,
or hoof it instead and avoid the fuss.

He'd earned his right to do nothing much,
to have lots of time to fill.
To sit tight, without shame.
9.30 already. Curtains swept apart,
a charcoal vista start – again.

Setting the mood for the day.
One of those.
Wash, breakfast, mobilise, organise.
Don't think – gets you nowhere,
that slope is steep; don't go that way.

Not quite raining, yet; raincoat of course.
Back pack, key, out the door, into Zen,
not too slow or fast.
It's now getting on for half-past,
ten.

By noon he's back,
but it's still not right.
He could not find his dream state.
Maybe later; perhaps tonight.
He felt it was a day to go over the pond.

Book in hand he set off,

across the road; busy now, impatient drivers.

Over the little arch bridge,

then past the old boating hut.

Quiet. Sacred serenity; except for his cough.

Towards his usual spot, far end of the little lake;

his bench. On the way he stops.

Looking down into the water; still, opaque,

he sees reflections of life's confections.

Don't think. Feel, but don't think.

A crack in the cloud, perhaps sunshine,

later. Comforting to see.

Reading about other places, again.

Mexico this time;

where writers tell stories of 'Magical Reality'.

Sitting there on his bench he could see how.

Listening to the delicious trickle of the melt,

from the brook behind – in the wood.

Everything is happening as it should;

he felt.

Winter is for all a test,

he must endure, just like the rest.

An upward glance, the sun is out;

he'd best go home and take the washing off the line.

It will be dark soon about.

By the time he'd walked a while along,

it was the middle of May.

It was still not dark; the sky was blue, not grey.

And that was definitely a Yellowhammer,

with its 'little bit of bread and no cheese' song.

How was this possible, he thought.

How much had he missed; was it an imaginary call?

Or could it be the enchantment of the pond,

that caught.

Perhaps he was in his dream state, after all...

Replay

Can it ever be the same?

Try again and hope it can be nursed.

But no, this time still differs from the first.

We wonder if we did it as we did before..

It's not as once it might have been.

We long to know how this indeed is so.

Could it be that life is just a drain.

Down which ourselves we desperately pour..

Perhaps it's best to play it all once more.

Enduring such exquisite throbbing pain.

So to ensure we never pass this way again.

Yet no one knows what future holds in store..

Each event is unique to the core.

And yet the track replays, it will not wane.

To spend resources sweet, and not regain.

Is there an entry or perhaps an exit door?

The Door

The Door

There is no hiding place.
The room is an echo chamber for thoughts,
when the door is closed.

Cast in muted grey.
Memories chase each other around the walls,
in delusional detachment.

Regressive enclosure.
Each corner distorting struggles from the past;
throw backs in the mind.

To that which is done.
Set in mental theatre, embedded deep inside;
acrid versions of the old.

There is air and light.
The pressure eases off to stay and fight,
when the door is open.

Outside is the future.
As yet unwritten in this closet of a mind,
it could be fine.

Around is still the same,
but now diluted, somehow, by the frame;
a vision of conceit.

Out there is incomplete.
Where was a door, is now perhaps a path,
to what might be.

Tomorrow.
The light shines in with beams of hope and risk;
all is not yet done.

Everything is cleansed with colour.
The hour is late, but life's candle is still drawn,
to what is new.

One day I will step through.

I Think Not

What does it take to kill a soul?

A question no one thinks to ask.

Perhaps after all, it's too close to home,

or even too near the fragile zone.

Everyone must wonder at some time or other.

How long does it last?

Can you poison, knife or shoot it,

or will it succumb to heavy military force?

Maybe disease will get it, in due course.

Some say that boredom can do the trick.

While others argue this thing within

is protected by faith, or absence of sin.

But no. I think not.

It must be that to kill a soul,

requires only the absence of love.

Of No Return

There is the terrifying thunder,

with its awe inspiring lightening.

Then there is the gentle purring;

of the cat.

The vicious verbal clawing,

striking home, yet spark eroding.

While the dog is sleeping soundly;

on the mat.

In the embers of the screaming,

and impotency of crying,

comes the deepening solemnity;

of peace.

This shedding of all loathing,

and the sadness underlying,

can reveal the joy of happiness;

release.

If we could only somehow pause,

and not embrace the hate filled troping,

then perhaps we could be free;

before the point.

Making The Beast

Most pleasant silky sweaty ride,
displaced by lassitude on ebb tide.

The servile violence has now been done,
ambivalent nature may choose to flow.
As raging torrents can follow the sun,
so also, in time, might new seed grow.

Duhkha

To let you go, and so to set you free, from me.

That you can live and breathe untied,

reborn into the human sea.

Our song is sung, no longer drawing joyful tear

though play as play we tried;

it's true I know, yet sadly do I fear.

We must for peace of mind reach out

and together close on us the door.

This last remains to bring about;

it can be my love, alas, no more.

Distressed Green

Don't mess with me,

there's just no way I'll take it.

If you try and push your luck,

you'll be sorry; I don't fake it.

Don't flirt or trawl,

I'm not the kind to crumble.

If you muck about at all,

I won't fart around or fumble.

Don't wet your pants,

but I can hurt you if I have to.

If you so much as cast a glance,

I'll bend you 'till I break you.

Don't play that card,

or I'll put you in your place.

If you sniff around the yard,

I'll rearrange your pretty face.

So don't fuck with me,

or I'll have to bring you down.

You don't want to take me there,

I'm the hardest girl in town.

He Knows

When she nervously twirls his ring on her finger,
while smiling sweetly as he comes in close;
he knows.

When she casts her eyes down and not into his,
sitting coolly aside in that way that she can;
he knows.

Could he be wrong, is it all in his head,
might she just be dreaming of him instead?

But when her glance betrays that flicker of guilt,
the silent code seeps down into his soul;
he knows.

Over the years he'd searched deep within,
should he have lingered, or let her go?
Now he knows.

Who Can Say

But there's always hope if things go bad.
If life won't go the way you planned.
Or even if you just turned sad.

Don't let it go; that ray of gleaming possibility.
That silver band of true belief; no one can know.
There is no inevitability.

Don't tire and fall and wish it all away.
Hold fast; stay on the upward slope.
It could all change another day.

For if it's dark, you could make it light.
And if it's wrong, you could make it right.

Who can say?

Going Wrong

A hiccough in life,

a small crisis, nothing more.

We read about such things by the score.

Interweb advice a-plenty.

And yet still troubled and uncurled,

I was looking for the centre of my world.

I consulted a helpful stranger,

and engaged the Buddha in my search.

To find an answer to my philosophical lurch.

Until, at last, it came to me

that all along, there was nothing wrong.

It was simply the way that life had gone.

Knowing this I could once more dare.

In fact, I already had the tools.

It seems we are adequate, or we are fools.

Garden Fence Blues

His back garden fence is broken once more,
leaning bravely against the fierce wind and hoar.
It's happened each winter for year after year,
just screened by the Laurel, out of sight, way back here.

The short fence to the side was a problem to tell,
one Christmas it wobbled and teetered, then fell.
With the beginning of spring, he did the right thing;
   at long last,
and replaced it with new, so it could take a good blast.

Across his back fence, the posts are still strong,
when they crumble he'll change those as well, all along.
But for now he'll continue to cobble and repair,
his long suffering back fence; all five panels, out there.

He knows the forces of nature must win in the end,
as he bends his tired back; his old fence to defend.
Yet he wishes sometimes he had no fence at all;
in fact, he'd prefer a solid brick wall.

Ted

Ted

Our little Ted is looking over at us.
From the bed we can see him sitting there without a fuss.
His charity shop smile says 'don't mess with me',
but he's as soft as a brush, well, as soft as Ted can be!
From his post atop the sideboard, we know he can peer,
out through the window, but we've never seen him near.

Ted looks after the house when we're off and away,
to warmer places in winter for a longish stay.
When we return he's exactly where he was before,
waiting for us to decide when we'll go away some-more.
It's almost as though while we've been absent from home,
he's moved not an inch, just like a garden gnome!

But that's not the case as he's been wandering about,

on his security patrol, he's a very good scout.

We know this is true as in the kitchen below,

he gets bread and milk in, should we decide to show.

(There's a rumour it's really Sue's Dad, but we think this

a bit thin,

as Ted, for sure, would never let him in!)

Right now we're back home and as I'm lying here in bed,

he's behind a flower vase, out of sight; poor old Ted.

A Peach

I will admit, I'm not too good at much.
Perhaps I'm not good at anything at all,
but I believe I'm good at some things, just.
Though I overthink and then, of course, I stall.

Most of us are fairly good at something.
A few even spot a nice seductive niche,
by lucky chance just floating on the wing.
The joy of this must be sweeter than a peach.

The Box

It's a box I keep inside me,
to be precise, inside my head.
It's under lock and key,
so I sleep soundly in my bed.

There's no perfect human being,
no one out there who's sublime.
Mistakes are made for want of seeing,
some of which may hurt in time.

There were many times it's true,
when I suffered with the rest.
But where to put the residue,
and not put others to the test.

There's a method through the madness,

a cure perhaps for this malade.

I pack the anguish and the sadness,

in a place just for the bad.

All the pain and all the strife,

all the hurting, grief and fears.

All the worst things in my life

I place inside; and dry my tears.

My Phone and I

I'm in love with my phone.

We often go to bed together.

Sometimes, when I ask, my phone says;

'not tonight – I have a...low battery'.

We are intimate, my phone and I.

I take her everywhere I go.

My phone knows me best.

I think my phone knows me better than I know myself.

But the frustrating moments get me down a bit.

Consummation is what I crave, but she remains aloof.

Late at night, when I need her most,

my phone often feels a low battery coming on.

I am wondering if, after all,

my phone does not love me.

Perhaps I am being played along.

No matter; I am faithful to my miniature miracle.

She often has data problems now, and more often

backing-up issues on videos.

She also complains that I do not purchase presents,

increasingly advertised on her screen.

But we will stay together…

Until an attractive new model should come my way.

Perhaps It's Love

Perhaps it's love,

when you yearn for someone else.

Perhaps it's love,

when your heart beats till it melts.

Perhaps it's love,

when you cannot find the words.

Perhaps it's love,

when you're singing like the birds.

Perhaps it's love,

when you share what's good and bad.

Perhaps it's love,

when she's happy, yet you're sad.

Perhaps it's love,

when you know that she'll be there.

Perhaps it's love,

when you know for sure she'll care.

Maybe it's love,

when that cold place in your heart,

is warmed up with hope and joy,

in that exciting brand new start.

Maybe it's love,

when you cannot get your fill,

of that sweet and lovely girl,

who looked at you and said 'I will'.

Maybe it's love,

when you bring children to the world.

When you know forever more,

your two lives will be en-twirled.

Maybe it's love,

when, no matter where you are,

you know there's someone there.

Whether near or far.

Perhaps these types are all the same,

or each one a different kind.

But if you're a lucky man,

perhaps all of them you'll find.

Ruffle

I have a weakness; I'll admit to at least one.

Like other people, I'm only flesh and blood.

There, I've said it.

Now it's done.

Sometimes it's strong and then I crave.

Sometimes I fight it off, though I'm not brave.

But other times it's just too hard,

so I concede and crumble like a low value card.

I know it's wrong,

that it's not good for me.

But, regretfully, I do it anyway;

sometimes day after day.

I can't seem to find a way out of this
delightful dilemma; bountiful bliss.
It's been with me now for sixty years,
a mix of pleasure, surrender and guilty fears.

So I think I'm resigned to living with it,
on my habits, with age, I'll more easily sit.
Whatever the case, I'll go near or far,
for a raspberry ruffle chocolate bar.

That Train   (For Jilly)

I must admit to feeling guilt,
but I enjoyed it to the hilt.
From the city of love with my older sis,
to the beautiful place that is my Venice.

I won a prize changing tyres no less,
couldn't believe my luck, I must confess.
Two tickets for me to take the ride,
so I'll have my sister by my side.

'Surprise surprise' said I to Joy,
'do come on the train with me.
We'll be on the express, yes the Orient one.
Oh Joy, oh boy oh boy.'

First to get up to London town,
to meet up at Joy's place and plan our course.
I knew full well that we'd both enjoy,
this famously glamorous tour-de-force.

It was sad we couldn't take Nan as well,
that this difficult choice to me befell.
So we didn't tell my other sister then,
it would only have upset her yet again.

Set out early for Waterloo, not to miss
our carriage awaiting in sweet Paris.
'Don't forget we'll be dressing up big sister,
you might just meet a handsome mister.'

At dinner that night we were sat in our frocks,
the men were all formal with scotch on the rocks.
All the tables were laid in that luscious saloon,
we were served with the first course, tastefully soon.

Then at the end of the car the piano broke in;
such a beautiful tune with the tonic and gin.
'I could be no happier' said I with a wink,
'Not even when I met the Queen, I think.'

It was a wonderful trip, we both agreed,
we'd never forget That Train.
To have had the chance to go just once,
was a dream come true, in the main.

But long after the trip Nan said to me,
'Have you been on That Train yet?'
I didn't have the heart to say we had,
it would only have made her feel bad.

Books

I am, I'm sure, weighed down by books.
A room given over to hard and soft,
is getting full, maybe convert the loft.

This mountain formed itself behind my back,
I'm sure of that.
While I was immersed inside the outside world.

I love books, I'm sure you can tell.
I love their feel, their texture, their mystery, their smell.
Their latent promise of 'somewhere else'.

I have many books. I have too many books.
But, and this might be the thing:
Once a book is read, is it dead? And if not, what then?

When my mind has 'uploaded' the book,

and I have 'consumed' the text within,

this little world should go in the bin.

Or Should it?

Often, I take a book not read for years,

then 'consume' it once again;

a renewal of its treasure of thrills and tears and fears.

Once more new to me; almost.

For there is nothing in life like that first time.

But I am a faithful soul, right down the line.

So I am still weighed down with my books.

Culture Trolls

Out there the air was New World fresh,
not stale like our anaemic breath.
A life of futures beaconed us,
just customise our old world fuss.

We went and then came back again,
the Devils here we thought we'd slain.
But no, it's not turned out that way,
they won't yield now or any day.

While kicking hard to cast them off,
we held us close to ward off loss.
It must be true they never leave,
at every turn in us they breathe.

Residing not out there somewhere,
within, that's where they build their lair.
So we nurse the remains of our child-like souls,
as we age less bold; with our Culture Trolls.

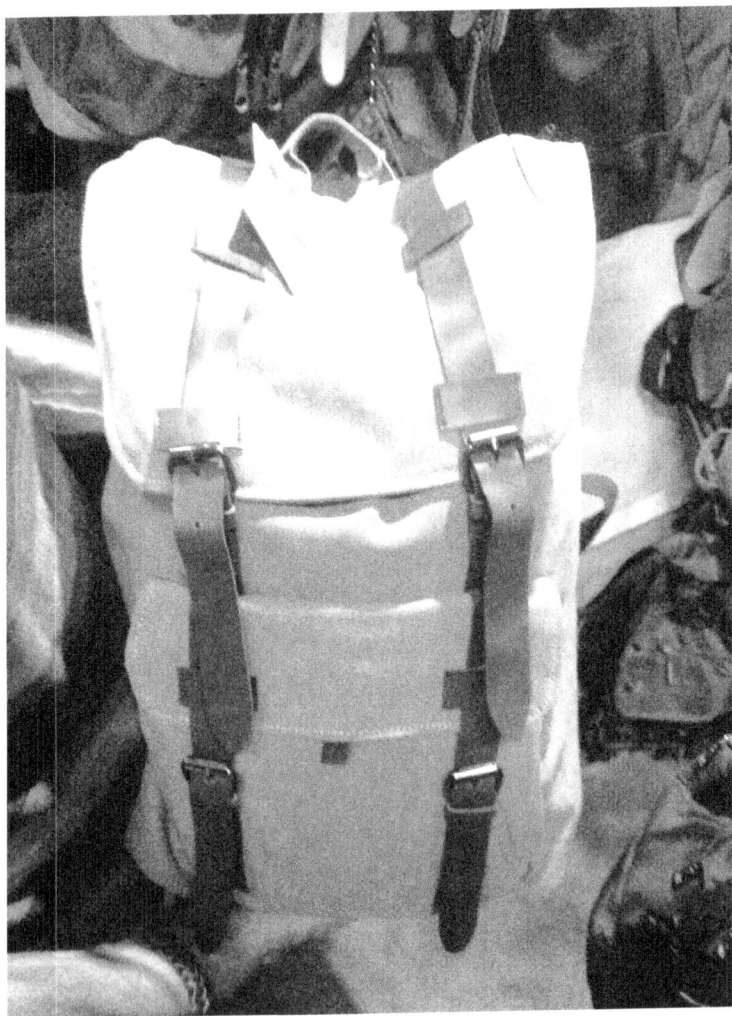

Leaving Again

Leaving Again

The West Australian sun holds court
on my world, as it did long before.
The Fremantle Doc with relieving forte,
blows its Indian Ocean encore.

Beautiful honeyed people still play
on the beaches, so lovely and clean.
Each body a youthful temple, just like
some kind of Shakespearian dream.

As I cast back through a deepening mist
searching for an Elysian note.
I'm here on this coast with its natural twist,
not then so obscure, or remote.

Under my feet is the sensuous sand

baking hot, so I cool in the spray.

Sweet liaison between the sea and the land

makes my reverie special this day.

Though my ageing dream-time call is met

by a receding and distant reply,

the spring in my step means I'll never regret

I was here; but for now I must fly.

The Village

It was so clearly different,
and yet it seemed the same;
this special place I remember well.
More than forty years of life I'd spent
until, once more, I came.

Some things remained as I recall,
the humble block of back-packer rooms;
ours with the Gecko pic still on the wall.
Though of course much else was changed,
as the overlay of Western infusion looms.

Near the beach, where once was sand,

lay a smart new restaurant in the modern style;

with aircon', designed for a comfortable stay.

All minimalist girders, and so sterile;

for the discerning bule on their fortnight away.

No longer then, as it was before.

But the beating heart persists apace;

these graceful people are its tropic core.

With Lombok to the east and all the world beyond the reef,

in tranquil time and space.

Blowing It

It was so nearly mine.
I could smell the scent of new life,
like sweet lilies in a pond.

Just an inch or two, no more.
The feeling now immense,
I'm no longer living on the fence.

Then all around seems changed.
In place of ecstasy grows fear,
as the point of no return comes near.

Doubts invade my mind.
Perhaps I can no longer learn,
this dream of mine must surely burn.

Elation now defaced with pain.
Too much; I bend and break,
for fear it's all a fools mistake.

It's over, it's undone.

Play in safe mode my mind is told,

my new life lapses back on hold.

For now.

The feeling has returned.

I am emboldened yet again,

to place my hand over the flame.

And this time hold it there.

For this new life to be a fit,

I must endure and fight for it.

That is only fair.

The Anchor

Without it I'd be gone by now,
without a care, to who knows where.
A good thing or perhaps a bad,
is it better to think or just to dare?
Best not to dwell or we'll all go mad.

Good holding's what we mostly need,
is commonly thought and often said.
All well and good for staying put,
snug in your warm and comfy bed.
There may be storms, best check the hook.

But if the pick should shift, what then,
do we drift with wind and tide prevailing?
Would that be such an awful thing?
Maybe now it's time to rig for sailing;
to take a chance and see what fate may bring.

Bumps In The Road

Finding the strength,
I had journeyed so far.
Time to let you be,
who you really are.

So young for the light,
to be turned into dark.
In that very cold place,
deep inside a lost heart.

But all you would have felt,
were the bumps in the road.
We two went unnoticed,
no need to lighten the load.

Softer

I feel I'm getting softer,
as the years unfold away.
I sense things much more deeply,
as I pass through life's affray.

Yet as far as I can see,
not all people are this way.
Some turn out, it seems to me,
harder with each passing day.

So, one way or another,
people just don't stay the same.
Like the leaving of a lover,
transformation grows from pain.

Perhaps I should get tougher,
but my nature won't permit.
Instead, I'll just avoid the rougher,
and progress my gentle trip.

Innermost Outside

It is a conceit perhaps to think,
that at poetry one can play.
But is it conceited really,
to open up to the light of day?

Seeping thoughts from one mind
set down; from such a flow
defragmentation must surely grow.
Or at least release the untold.

Exposure, though perverse to know,
appeals. Attractive openness,
shear nakedness the goal. To dare
cast shadows from one raging soul.

And so a private public space
emerges, from emotion in reframe.
Feelings set down in their ordered place
look up, now living on the page.

Zen

It's all a beautiful blur.

The sun never sets on that island.

Everything I didn't do for you,

is still yours.

I knew you had been there.

I felt the warmth of the sun on your skin.

A silver lining, so crystal clear,

like the fall of a raindrop.

It rains softly, just looking at you.

The clear eastern sky holds the moment,

my heart stopped by.

On my journey to mindfulness.

Frangipani

Frangipani

There is always a scent to miss; a sensuous kiss.

Humans smell.

It's a pity, but there it is.

First thing in the morning,

before the sun escapes his night time lair.

When the fertile tropic growth

is not yet captured by the intense solar glare.

Appear two palms across the narrow path,

now intimately entwined.

Grown so close they must sway as one,

as if by fate they are eternally assigned.

A fragile moment, wafer thin,

with fecund bouquets of Bali cast around.

Hibiscus, Bougainvillea and Jasmine,

can all be found.

Amid this throng the Frangipani balm seems strong,

as does a woman who is bad.

And also lasts perhaps as short or long,

though incense sweet, is yet so very sad.

Is there in this a subtle beauty deep,

a golden glimpse maybe, of something lost or sought?

Before man rises from his sweaty shallow sleep

and, without so much as witnessing or thought

Lights up; exhaling toxic musk upon it all,

destroying what for him, with her,

could never have been caught.

Buds

Between the petals is where
the true story resides.
Though the writing is bare,
fragrance never lies.

Just look above and below
the dried folds of cold ink.
Undressing beauty to show,
forgotten sorrow and stink.

To the left and right hide
coded secrets which tell.
When we blossomed then died,
how we leaped and then fell.

The silent scent of each day
in the passage of years.
That's where the memories lay,
of both the joy and the tears.

At the end breathing sighs,
exquisite honesty rubs
the facade from old lies.
Revealing tender new buds.

The Fabric Of Life

So the weave unfolds,
when its warping rends.
The thread of passion erodes,
into a state of 'good friends'.

Shuttling down the line,
there's a thrumming of age.
The living texture of time,
incites the soul to enrage.

How sad, some project,
as the loom turns stone cold.
But wise heads may detect,
subtle yarns yet untold.

Fraying edict to breed,

with its jealous discord.

The crude pattern of need,

can at last be ignored.

Still Universe matter,

though somehow more awake.

Now unbound from life's clatter,

to re-bond; not truncate.

I Have Noticed

I have been noticing of late,
that the days are so much longer.
And that I am falling down,
in my consideration of you.

I may ask of you a question,
the summer sun is now on high.
Then fail to listen to your reply.
'I'm sorry, I didn't hear you', I lie.

Neglectful of small comments,
the clouds above may blow away.
As my mind is wandering astray
you feel, perhaps, a little in the way.

In my world I can be selfish,
closed off from our inner space.
Until I see you drop your head:
'It hurts both you and me', I said.

You Shall Not A Victim Be

But you shall not a victim be,
all paths leads there, 'tis sad but true.
The hurt in life is plain to see,
though not I hope, my love, for you.

Yet shielding you is my domain,
cast harm away from mind and soul.
To cut out painful mortal stain,
intense my need to keep you whole.

When I should fail to so fulfil,
may devil's angels haunt my rest.
Until my breath be also still,
 with you in our eternal nest.

Lifting The Weight

I mean no harm, I say with pain,
or hurt to you in any way.
I strive to bridge the yawning gap
through inner conflict, but not with you.
Regret just seems to draw the sap,
no golden words from me will rain.

Such weakness in unvarnished form
is what you see. We both despise
this loathsome load, and hate
its wretched, two-faced guise.
Yet still I try to lift the weight,
and wish this part of me unborn.

Once more to sink back in defeat. I say again,
I mean no harm, or hurt to you, in any way.

Your Image

We can no longer be as one,
but our embrace continues still.
This race it seems is not yet run,
as we progress life's ageing mill.

A wonder then; this thing of ours
which enthrones no body proud.
That all for us be as with flowers
uncut, though yield from ground.

Deep mystery true, my hold on you,
this spell that grips us tight.
Amazing is this magic glue,
too strong for us to fight.

And yet what binds us to our vows,
in seductive 'we' not 'I'?
Perhaps for me that which allows,
your image where I lie.

Stardust In Time

As we twist and we turn through the habits of life,

there's no rhythm or rhyme to the struggle and strife.

Precious moments in time as we go, lock in place,

giving stardust and light to the toil that we face.

But there's no waiting to ponder the point of it all,

as we rush on headlong to the ultimate call.

I Would Not

The skies could start to fall,
the floods wash everything away.
To collapse beneath us all.
But I would not.

We could drink our merry way,
towards an ever growing darkness.
Or work into an early grave.
But I would not.

Old father time could rot and decay,
the timber deep inside our houses.
All could be lost and cast away.
But I would not.

The cold could freeze in us
our bones, until the flesh distend.
The howling wind could blow and gust,
until what could be bent, would bend.

But I would not.

Uncrushed

But it did not sit well with him.
His voice was like thunder as,
raising his arms to the heavens,
he said:

'I have not been erased,
or swept away from this earth.
Nor am I deleted,
I'm still here and about.
I am not disappeared,
or somehow vanished from sight.
Here I stand, big and bold,
in my place; dark or light.'

In defiance, it seemed, of time itself.
He was seen, he was heard,
and though impotent,
his strength was respected.

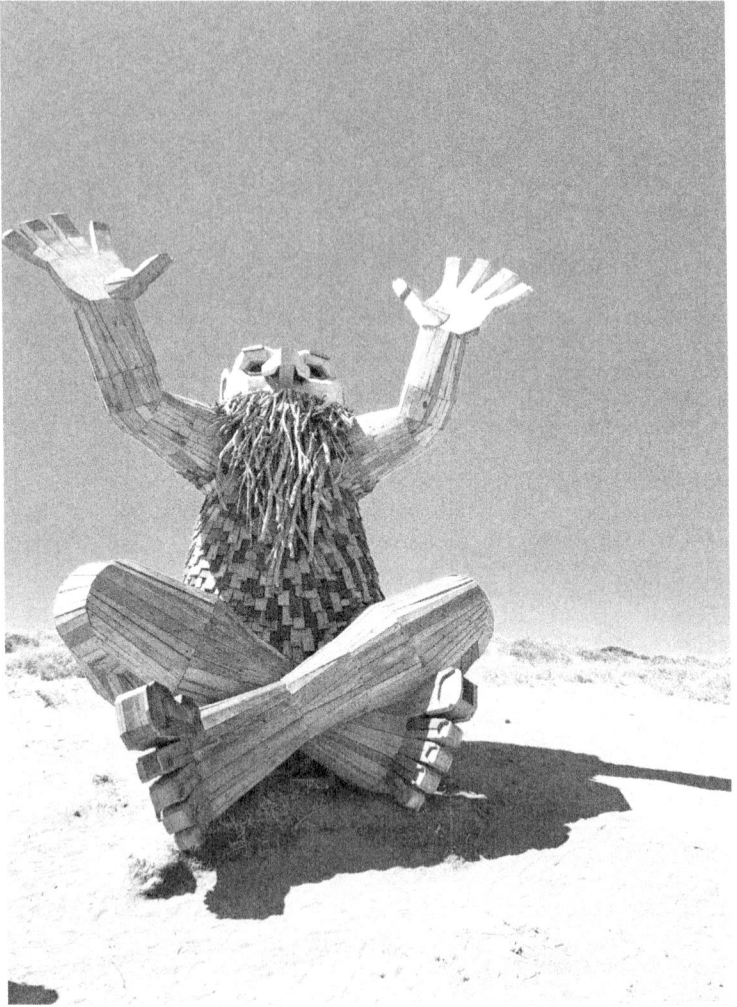

The Giant Man

Don't Shut Down

To speak the truth yet be denied,

bear witness false that you had lied.

Embrace no wrong nor cast out right,

inflict no pain without insight.

Under such weight might someone drown,

but it can't happen if you don't shut down.

The Fates

He knew it had to be this way,
he could have fought it day by day.
He felt that it might never end,
the fates decreed it would never mend.

The point is lost in such a mess,
he knew full well, no need for stress.
There comes a time when it's enough.
The fates decide such things for us.

The writing's clear upon the wall,
it's there to see for one and all.
It's no one's fault, not then or now,
The fates you see just won't allow.

Not Fade To Grey

When you become an older man,
people start to think you no longer can
do all that young folk find to do;
please fade to grey without further ado.
With wrinkled face and greying hair,
it's considered that you need extra care.

An older man just will not fit
into life's joys, he's done his last trick.
His struggle is over, now it's the time
to sit back and enjoy an encroaching decline.
He cannot hide the advancing years,
which confirm his most impotent fears.

At this age the girls still look very pretty;
perhaps even more, though the hormones are bitty.
They look at him not as a male,
but more like he's too far down the trail.
Yet he feels the same as he always did,
maybe with more calm and a lot less glib.

There's confusion mixed with clarity,

as life lends him new eyes to see

the impressive latest crop of young.

Of which he is no longer one.

Some gratefully drop into Grandparent role,

still needed, though on the reproductive dole.

For other types this just will not do.

They need to find a new challenge to glue

the purpose back on to a sagging life.

They will not quit, they'll pay the price.

The sandman's not yet come for them,

so until that time;

    they'll behave like men.

Hiding In The Past (The Mushroom)

There's a lot of it about these days,

it's mostly my generation, and our fickle ways.

A backward looking lot we turned out to be,

without even a thought for the blatant hypocrisy.

It's the 'mushroom bulge' we're told; a blip, a one off blast.

There were many of us 'boomers' born in those distant

  post-war years,

then the pill came by to set us free and calm our loving fears.

So we didn't need to breed like other cohorts in the past.

You see 'in our day', when we were fit and young,

we laughed at older people for not having had much fun.

Their stories of 'the war' we thought were boring, in a way,

Dad's Army wasn't comedy but a parody of them 'in their day'.

The 1960's saw 'the generation gap' develop in the West;

our mob defined modernity, and we of course knew best.

Progressive ideology had won, or so we arrogantly thought,

but over time the past crept in until, eventually, up it caught.

Members of our 'permissive society' were indulgent to
   the core,
in freedoms undreamt-of by those who'd gone before.
We showed scant regard for older ways or parental concern,
with establishment values despised at each and every turn.
Over time these keys to liberty have been fondly handed
   down,
for future generations to enjoy; you might assume.
Except of course they haven't; as even a cursory look,
shows the conservative boot fits nicely on the baby-boomer
   foot.

Now it's the young and not the old who must tolerate all
   our mores,
pandering to our needs and cares with bygone social laws.
The kids are chaperoned to within an inch of our own fears,
they are never left unsupervised as our big-brother culture
   steers.
And growing to maturity, where can they turn to live?
With the oldies? Why of course, for yet more childhood with
   us bores.
Most aspire to adulthood and that's all well and good,
but can't reach that independence for which we once proudly
   stood.

The entertainment world is filling up with replay and revision,

sentimental overdubbing of the 'glorious' past, in Panavision.

While our youth are cast away on the Brexit ship of fools,

we're busy blaming others, not our own political tools.

As we age into our parents, now Dads Army seems to fit,

but not to worry on our arses we, as usual, comfortably sit.

We have our nicely indexed pensions, paid for homes and free
  healthcare,

though, on second thoughts, the NHS is nigh beyond repair.

The mushroom bulge has now matured and we've had our
  wicked way,

even though we've definitely had an over-longish stay.

Denim uniforms long gone, forgotten figments in the head,

shut the light off, if you're last into the lucky boomer bed.

It's fair to say degeneration should mostly take the blame,

for the way the world turned out in our ageing sorry train.

All in all, we've done a thorough job on those who follow on,

but even now most aren't aware; we sold it all for a populist
  song.

The Few

How much space do we need?

How much more do we crave?

Is it not just avarice or greed,

to worship not the noble but the naive?

Is it worth what must be drawn in blood?

While insisting others owe the debt.

Once begun we won't curtail the flood,

until emerges from the pain a 'winning' set.

Is there enough in this to pay,

for sacrifice of lives forever gone?

Can slaughter really be the only way,

or would a coin toss save our youthful song?

Still better, could all those who lead,

with claims that killing must be done anew.

Forfeit their lives, therefore themselves to bleed,

and this time save the many, not the few.

Rage

Where speaks a rage without pain or hurt,
nor sadness or even fear of loss.
There speaks a rage of chastened pride,
of status ebb; ego in its stride.

This type reveals a loss of face,
perhaps a hint of grim disgrace.
If rage it be which claims the day,
beware this route which leads astray.

Such rage can change the set of things,
from what may be to what may not.
Once tightly bound the coil unwinds,
the force released then often blinds.

But worst of all reveals the self,
once hidden; buried deep within.
Becomes exposed to those outside;
the rider brought down by the ride.

Ugly (circa 2016-2024)

Perhaps you may think that it's not very pretty,

to see our elites bring us down; such a pity.

Perhaps you may sense that it's one holy mess,

that we're heading towards the 'third-world'; more or less.

Ticked the wrong box and there's no hope in sight,

heading straight for what's wrong while ignoring what's right.

With illness, division and poverty up,

are we now in a sickening spiralling rut?

A taste of the future feels sad and contrite,

seeing youngsters to come living property 'lite'.

Resources depleted, pollution sky high,

while our race still expands we seem deaf to earth's cry.

Perhaps we can ease the distress of a few,

but there's no going back, we must face it anew.

If all this rings true it may be we can help.

Let's back the grown-ups;

and climb out of the fantasy stew.

Difference   (UK, summer, 2024)

'It's racism pure and simple'
someone recently said to me,
about the riots in UK towns and cities.
But how has this all come to be?

It's a tribal thing, I firmly believe,
I felt it almost at my mother's knee.
There was 'our' group and also 'other' groups
living quietly, peacefully and free.

The other groups were a little mysterious, I would say;
a few Jewish and black people mostly, as I recall.
But nothing was 'their fault' yet, around our way.
There was also a community of Catholics.

The Catholics have churches and schools of their own
in a semi-apartheid arrangement, they appear to prefer.
Adults in our tribe didn't bother about this much,
but accepted the 'other' as partly home-grown.

I noticed also at roughly this time,

the depiction of Christ in our places of prayer.

He always seemed light, no, I would say 'white'.

I wondered a little, but it was still fine.

When I was older, I saw a globe of the world.

There was much British pink on this cast of the past.

To their credit, some teachers would let us all know,

most history is written by winners, especially long ago.

Alongside the English and Maths, we were taught

of the Romans, and how slaves were sold and bought.

Since the British Empire was big in its day,

our values were spread widely, it seems fair to say.

We played our part in exporting the blight.

Ideas were transported with some of our kin;

of difference, 'free' markets and hierarchy of skin.

So Jesus, I suppose, had to be white, or at least light.

But I had a friend with a dark shade of skin.

A 'mixed marriage' child;

white father, black mother, his dad had one arm.

We knew that they struggled, with little money coming in.

Just like us, they paid the 'council house' rent
for their post-war home, built in the 'baby boom' years.
So they were part of our tribe in a significant way.
Ours was a comfy two bed; inside loo, heaven sent.

At school assembly, we sometimes sang hymns;
belting out 'Jerusalem' as though it was quite near.
But that place I knew to be much further away
and it was certainly not 'builded here'.

The years have gone by and the globe is less pink,
but our 'cultural imprint' still exists in some forms.
Our migrated 'creation myth', if you will, is a link.
Such stories are found in the world's tribal norms.

As an Australian migrant I was afforded respect,
yet I noticed an 'out' group existed even there.
Aboriginal Peoples, some thought, were 'low cast' in effect,
but light skins were fine, even when far worse for wear.

This immoral assumption, a cultural trap,
told of our ancient values not yet melted away.
For I never was witness to treatment like that
about white people invited down under to stay.

But I think Australians, especially the young,

have now come to terms with this sorrowful past.

What our backwardly slanting transporting had done,

and First Nationals had then undergone.

So much older and back in my country of birth,

I see the toxic results of 'hard-right' ways.

In riots brought on by the 'mythical home-land' thugs,

and the climate of fear from this violence craze.

At Brexit time, I thought for a moment, perhaps it was me.

Did I miss the point? But no, the feudal gates were opened
  wide

to our racist fellow travellers, egged on by those who
  shamelessly lied.

Unleashed upon us now, inspired by those who would not see.

By the way, I'm white; as if it didn't make a difference.

A Migrant's Prayer

Thank you, oh Lord, for bestowing on me,
the wonderful gift of trans-nationality.
Through the migration conduit which I have been sent,
I'm learning to live in the moment; unbent.

I know very well that you have not granted
the leave for so many to be likewise replanted.
But some, perhaps many, are too firmly entrenched,
in the ways of their place; with teeth fully clenched.

For those I wish wisdom to cultivate,
a vista not seen through the prism of hate.
With no sense of fear, to discover instead,
the power and the freedom of movement; not dread.

Unveiling the colour and even the creed

of such travellers as us, for like you, we all bleed.

Perhaps those who are blighted and narrowed this way,

can one day perceive what is false; and belay.

Misunderstanding is born of a simple unknowing,

which in turn is the father of prejudice sowing.

Knowing the artist may show us the picture,

let's pray this is part of our cultural mixture...

Amen

Ours Alone

Each one apart has dreamed of the past,

yet together we dance to the future.

What's gone is over and then, at last,

that which remains must be purer.

Those earlier times we each set aside,

in the quest for what belongs just to us.

The moments to come on this golden ride,

becoming special as we onward rush.

Until there is just one remaining,

with wings clipped sadly and youth now flown.

But the one remaining will cast back dreaming,

this time the past will be ours alone.

Alone

Too Tired To Be Free

Worn down by life, he feels his age,
long gone those days of storm and rage.
His body eroded by constant wear,
his mind confused by worry and care.

The years have passed, he's been too slow,
now time is become the biggest foe.
So tired of paying life's increasing fee,
he's afraid his escape might never be.

And yet he clings to what's still left,
deep down inside, not quite bereft.
By now it's just instinct; clean and pure,
to stay the course seems the only cure.

Resolved to break the bonds with flight,

to force his soul from visceral plight.

But his options have become few and slim,

to lift himself up from the grey and the grim.

He holds strong to the freedom that is found elsewhere,

not buried back home in a security lair.

So on a plane or a boat his hopes must rely,

to live out his dreams; or at least to try.

Replaceable

To find you are replaceable,

and not a special soul.

You're poured into a standard mould,

then tapped out oh so cold.

Into a world conditional,

on obedience sublime.

There's no debate, at any rate,

no quarter any time.

There are plenty out there off the peg,

no need for tailor made.

Just one mistake and in your stead,

another can be laid.

With luck you may have company,

a common thread or link.

Then you both could climb the freedom tree,

and grow instead of shrink.

There is alas, a lack of need

for one of such a pair.

Far better sure to let it bleed,

and find someone as rare.

Anonymous

He hides away from life,

and from any kind of strife.

Sliding silently by the weeks,

avoiding anyone in the streets.

Averting low his ageing head,

he passes by with gentle tread.

In case obliged to nod or speak,

he'd rather not, he's shy and meek.

Insecurely easing through,

over a softly printing shoe.

He's hoping just to get away

with being ignored again, today.

It's been a long and narrow life,

he rents a flat, never taken a wife.

Without a friend or mobile phone,

always alone, out on his own.

Except for once, back up the line,

there was a moment, sweet as wine.

He knew of course it couldn't last,

it quickly faded to the past.

Sipping quietly at the pub,

in a far corner, out of the rub.

Of human kind he seems afraid,

it's just the simple track he's laid.

To be anonymous is his aim,

his story's sad and very plain.

There are many of him out there,

so please be kind, don't stand and stare.

On Such A Day

One day, if you have any luck,

you might wake up and wonder;

'Is that it then' or 'Doesn't life suck'.

Strange this track that leads us under.

So where indeed do we really get?

Don't know who knows what it's all about.

You don't either, I'm willing to bet.

Nor what awaits us I very much doubt.

Religious people, with passionate phlegm,

tout their respective recruitment drives.

Extolling The Word, which lies only with them,

just follow the rules for much better lives.

But can all such doctrines be in the right?

By force of logic this cannot be so.

How then to know which casts the light,

are we left with nowhere else to go?

And what about the other creatures,

who make their way on this ball of blue?

Do we alone hold Godly features,

do they not deserve their holy due?

Recoiling then from image and idolatry,

towards instead a philosophical type.

Standing apart from all tribal bigotry,

a secular way must surely be right.

Some souls of course will never attain,

this pause to ponder the grand design.

Departing before such thoughts are in frame;

though forever young in hearts left behind.

A time then, perhaps, to embrace belief,

suspend what is true; conceal it away.

Accept invention to ease the grief,

as we nurse our sadness; on such a day.

Wings

The time has come, your wings are clipped,
no longer are you free to fly.
Instead you must embark the ship
of dreams, to help the days go by.

Stark truth appears, it's just as though
a vital link has upped and flown.
It seems this must indeed be so,
your summer leaves at last have blown.

With self-retrenchment, thus begins
a growing focussed inner world.
Where risks and even sordid sins
can flourish, new norms now uncurled.

An inwardly expanding space,
embalms the central core of life.
This unique increasing spectral place,
will ever more of you entice.

Outlook

Sitting here in heavy silence I see,
beyond the single glazed border of my world,
the Magnolia, looking up at me.

In my imaginings it is there only for me.
From the chair beside my bed, unslept,
I hoard its presence possessively.

The woven branches of my tree,
appear to me as twisted silver filigree.
Set in the hibernal frozen still.

The bedsit is cold. It has been that way forever,
but spring is near, or so I'm told.
Funny how the damp caresses.

The weight of winter presses down,
reducing us both in the living chain.
But my tree will shortly flower again,
and I have bloomed my last.

Not Yet

Perhaps there is a point at which we aim

and, when we thus attain,

this static journey will be broken

by its end

Much seems to be unchanged

wrapped in a cling-film cell

outside of time

Except for transformation

Not alone, just self-contained

with tales imprinted on the mind

A world of image and reality

always touching, some part of us

No, not of loneliness or even self-deception

but instead, of deep reflection

The enlightened 'I'

of dreams yet undefined

Reality

...The old man disappeared,

the one in the opposite flat.

The one who used to complain,

about the smell of my stray cat.

Went overnight, they say,

never noticed a thing.

He was the quiet sort anyway.

Didn't so much as say hello, at least not since last spring.

Yes, as I recall, he seemed to change just then;

didn't have a friend.

Dropped into his trance, again.

Left his washing on the line, for days on end.

Went for walks, would find a bench and quietly sit.

Didn't like to take the bus;

said once that it just didn't fit,

that he'd only catch one if he must.

But he had something about him,

a sense of mystery, perhaps.

As though he'd looked into the future

or seen the past suddenly collapse.

Don't know where he went or if he'll be back.

He was an other-worldly sort; a kind of gentle dreamer,

living deep outside of us.

In a way I'll miss him; I hear he didn't even pack.

The Brightening Light

Go recklessly into the brightening light,

do not succumb unto fear or flight.

Walk straight and tall with head held high,

let fate decide when it's time to die.

Meanwhile the gift is yours to grasp,

don't hide away till you breathe your last.

Instead, rejoice at life within,

for one day soon it will surely dim.

So go, go now, do not be afraid.

Heed not the darkening carefully laid

by those who surrender to morbid blight.

Be brave and reject that living night.

One Final Thought

It's time.

I feel it in my bones.

Just one more look around

in final consideration.

Of what has passed

in a lightening flash.

Seemingly without a sound.

There is an overwhelming calm

and even beauty,

of a kind.

I no longer need to run.

A serenity of moments

each and every one.

Is in me now, I find.

I'm there.

I don't know why

but I can tell.

Others must have felt it

when it was this way.

When it was time for them

as well.

There are no regrets

that it added up this way.

No fear, just wonder at the flow.

The pitter-patter

of little life drops.

Now softer.

It's time, at last, to go.

Words

It's a strange and abstract thing,

that often leads to who knows where.

But if you ride out on the rim,

you seem to fly without a care.

Just a series of small symbols,

marks upon a printed line.

As the storyline unfolds,

you're out of sight, and outside time.

Sadly everything must pass,

as with migrating flocks of birds.

The patterns set down here and cast,

passed through my mind, and are my words.

And now you have them too.

Also by Steve

Poetry collections:

- In The Moment   2021
- In Deep   2021
- In Transit   2022

An autobiographical account of emigration:

- A Ticket Out   2022

Published by

www.publishandprint.co.uk

Printed in Great Britain
by Amazon

47721805R00066